SHAPED BY SCRIPTURE

The Hope You Have

1 & 2 PETER

DAN BOONE

Copyright © 2023 by The Foundry Publishing®
The Foundry Publishing
PO Box 419527
Kansas City, MO 64141
thefoundrypublishing.com

978-0-8341-4127-8

Printed in the
United States of America

2

Cover Design: J. R. Caines
Interior Design: J. R. Caines
Layout: Jeff Gifford

The internet addresses, email addresses, and phone numbers in this book are
accurate at the time of publication. They are provided as a resource. The Foundry
Publishing does not endorse them or vouch for their content or permanence.

10 9 8 7 6 5 4 3 2 1

Contents

THE *SHAPED BY SCRIPTURE* SERIES

The first step of an organized study of the Bible is the selection of a biblical book that a reader plans to study. Often people pick a book they are most familiar with, or books they consider as easy to understand, or books that, according to popular opinion, have more relevance to Christians today than other books of the Bible. However, it is important to recognize the truth that God's Word is not limited to a few books. All the biblical books, both individually and collectively, communicate God's Word to us. As Paul affirms in 2 Timothy 3:16, "All Scripture is God-breathed and is useful for teaching, rebuking, correcting and training in righteousness." We interpret the term "God-breathed" to mean inspired by God. If Christians are going to take 2 Timothy 3:16 seriously, then we should all set the goal of encountering God's Word through all sixty-six books of the Bible. New Christians or those with little to no prior knowledge of the Bible might find it best to start with a New Testament book like 1 John, James, or the Gospel of John.

By purchasing this volume, you have chosen to study the books of 1 & 2 Peter. You've made a great choice because these two epistles offer the people of God words of wisdom for difficult times. They were written to help churches scattered across the Roman Empire remember God's mission and realign themselves with that mission. Because these books are short, they are perfect for a study like this one, whose goal is to illustrate an appropriate method of studying the Bible.

How This Study Works

This Bible study is intended for a period of seven weeks. We have chosen a specific passage for each week's study. This study can be done individually or with a small group.

For individual study, we recommend a five-day study each week, following the guidelines given below:

1 On the first day of the study, read the relevant passage several times until you become fully familiar with the verses, words, and phrases.

2 On the second day, we will review the setting and organization of the passage.

3 On the third day, we will observe some of the realities portrayed in the passage.

4 On the fourth day, we will investigate the relationship of the individual passage to the larger story of God in the Bible.

5 On the fifth day, we will reflect on the function of the story as we hear it today, the invitation it extends to us, and our response to God, who speaks through God's Word.

If this Bible study is done as a group activity, we recommend that members of the group meet together on the sixth day to share and discuss what they have learned from God's Word and how it has transformed their lives.

You may want
to have a study
Bible to give you
additional insights
as we work through
1 & 2 Peter. Other
helpful resources
are *Discovering the
New Testament* and
*1 & 2 Peter/Jude: A
Commentary in the
Wesleyan Tradition*,
both available
from The Foundry
Publishing.

Literary Forms in the Bible

There are several literary forms represented throughout the Bible. The divinely inspired writers used various techniques to communicate God's Word to their ancient audiences. The major literary forms (also known as genres) of the Bible are:

- narratives

- laws

- history

- Wisdom literature (in the form of dialogues and proverbial statements)

- poetry (consisting of poems of praise, lament, trust in God, and more)

- prophecy

- discourses

- parables

- miracle stories

- letters (also known as epistles)

- exhortations

- apocalyptic writings

Within each of these forms, one may find subgenres. Each volume in the *Shaped by Scripture* series will briefly overview the genres found in the book of the Bible that is the subject of that study.

When biblical writers utilized a particular literary form, they intended for it to have a specific effect on their audience. This concept can be understood by examining genres that are familiar to us in our contemporary setting. For example, novels that are comedies inspire good and happy feelings in their readers; tragedies, on the other hand, are meant to induce sorrow. What is true of the intended effect of literary forms in contemporary literature is also true of literary forms found in the Bible.

Introduction

1 & 2 PETER

When asked if he had ever been lost, American pioneer Daniel Boone replied, "No. But I was once bewildered for three days." That may be the best way to describe the state of the church of Jesus today—not exactly lost, but bewildered. We are trying to navigate Christian life in a changing world.

Our formation as the people of God is based on the belief that we are the elect, chosen by the Creator to reflect the image of Christ to the world. We exist for our neighbors, loving rather than conquering, being hospitable rather than defensive.

The way of Christianity is (or should be) different from the ways of worldly power. This makes the world see Christians as a threat. We find ourselves using language like "strangers" and "exiles" to describe our existence in the world. In cases like these, it is helpful to ask, "When have God's people been here before?"

One answer, of course, is the Babylonian exile. We find another answer in Peter's pastoral epistles. From the opening address of 1 Peter to the dispersed exiles, to the warnings in 2 Peter against false teachings, these letters seem to reflect our own context today.

Who Wrote 1 & 2 Peter?

The authorship of these two letters seems straightforward, since the writer is named in the first verses as Peter and Simon Peter, respectively. But scholars do not find the answer to be so simple. There are three common theories about the authorship of 1 Peter.

First, the writer may indeed be Peter, the apostle of Jesus who led the early church. In this case, the letter could be seen as his final instructions and evidence of his concern for the church as it spread beyond Jerusalem.

A second option is that it was written by Silas (or Silvanus), who served Peter. In this case, Silas could have written the words Peter dictated to him, used Peter's collected writings, or summarized Peter's thoughts. Summarizing an apostle's ideas was a task that servants commonly performed, whether during an apostle's lifetime or after the apostle's death. In this case, the letter would have Peter's name on it because it contained his ideas, even if someone else wrote them down.

A third possibility is that the letter was written by the "school of Peter." The early Christian community often formed schools that were similar to rabbinical schools in that they taught and trained students in the style of a specific teacher. The school of Peter could have existed well beyond the apostle's death and sought to continue his legacy by addressing the church in pseudonymous letters. In this case, the apostle's name would have given the letters authority, even if they were written after the beloved leader's death.

Second Peter seems less mysterious to scholars. It is more than likely pseudony-mous—written under Simon Peter's name by someone familiar with his teachings. (Not every pseudonymous book was accepted into the canon of Scripture—more were rejected than accepted.) A disciple could have written these letters from Rome after Peter's death in an attempt to warn the church against false teachings. Using Peter's name would have given the letter more authority. Scholars tend to agree that there are ample clues to suggest that the person who wrote 2 Peter is not the same person who wrote 1 Peter. Authorship questions notwithstanding, this study will refer to the author of both epistles as "Peter" for the sake of expediency.

These uncertainties about authorship should not affect our confidence in these important biblical epistles. We should remain open in our thinking where scholarship has not reached settled conclusions—it is not healthy for Christians to stake their claims of biblical authority on such issues. The primary question regarding the authority of Scripture is the way the Spirit speaks through it to the church. If we hear and obey the Spirit, then Scripture is authoritative for us.

Literary Form

Both 1 and 2 Peter are letters (or epistles) from a leader to several congregations, but we do not know if they were written to the same congregations. In fact, based on clues found in the texts, scholars think it is likely that they were written to and for different audiences. Both letters contain common features of first-century communication, including opening greetings, identification of the writer and intended readers, blessings, the raising of issues of concern, teachings, directives, and closing salutations.

Entering the Story

Reading an epistle is like overhearing one end of a phone conversation. We see what the writer says, but can only imagine what prompted the letter and how the recipients might have reacted. Yet the early church selected these letters for inclusion among the books of the Bible because they believed these words were for all believers everywhere. The Petrine epistles help the people of God understand their position in the world. While the issues in these letters are ancient, their implications are current for the church today. Therefore, we are among the intended recipients. The Holy Spirit is active in the gap between us and the text; we become actors engaged in the unfolding drama.

God speaks to us through the texts of the Bible so that we may be formed in the image of Jesus. When we see ourselves in the original audience, we hear the same Spirit who spoke to them also speaking to us. We can then offer the same obedience that God desired of the original readers. The Spirit is at work forming saints through our faithful obedience to God's revealed truth.

Major Theological Themes

The following themes form a theological framework for understanding the issues of 1 and 2 Peter.

We are divinely elected. The term "election" describes God's choice of Israel as a servant people through whom the world would be blessed. Jesus is the fulfillment of God's promises to Israel. Thus, Jesus's followers become God's elect people in the same way that Israel is, for the sake of witness.

We live in exile. We have little security as we live among powers that are suspicious of or hostile toward us.

We are eschatological travelers on the way to God's tomorrow. Eschatology is the doctrine that imagines our destiny—the future to which God calls us. Especially in these letters, this future is also called "the day of the Lord."

Some believers will defect from the faith. This issue has always been a cause for concern among God's people. From the worship of idols in the Old Testament to the compromises with pagan cultures in the New Testament, God's people are susceptible to defection.

Some believers will assimilate to the sinful culture. Many Christians never leave the faith, but compromise their devotion by failing to fully obey God.

Jesus is our model for Christian suffering. Jesus is the suffering servant of God who was prefigured in Isaiah. His example indicates that, as his followers, we too will endure suffering, and we too are empowered to glorify God through our suffering.

Some will try to lead us astray with false teachings. We should guard against teachings that sound good, but are not actually Christlike.

Scripture is our guidebook. New Testament audiences had the Old Testament to guide them, as well as the newly circulating stories about Jesus. Today, we have both testaments to teach and guide us.

Jesus is coming back. We should live like the second coming could happen at any moment. We anticipate Christ's return by living out God's mission and Christ's gospel in the world.

1 PETER 1:1–12

From the beginning to the end of 1 Peter, the primary metaphor for the people of God is *exiles*. Indeed, the book starts by calling them exiles in 1 Peter 1:1 (some translations read "exiles of the dispersion"). In 5:13, they are described as the elect brothers and sisters of God's people in Babylon (referring to the Old Testament exile story). Understanding this metaphor is essential to understanding the letter's function in the early church.

Old Testament Israel understood their exile in Babylon to be temporary. They lived in hope of going home. Their hearts yearned for the temple in Jerusalem, the songs of Zion, Jewish culture, and a Jewish calendar. Displacement was not just a temporary inconvenience, but a challenge to their identity. Surrounded by a pagan culture, they were at risk of assimilation. And indeed, throughout their history, Israel was prone to worship the gods of other tribes. Even if they did not renounce their faith in the God of Abraham, they often compromised that faith by adopting the ways of other gods and building altars to them. As their history attests, defection was in their genes.

This is why the exile metaphor is at the heart of this letter. The people of God are a threatened minority living in cities where God's ways are strange, and pagan powers surround them. Their identity is up for grabs; the pressure to compromise is relentless. Throughout history, God's people have always felt the dominant culture's pull. The book of 1 Peter is about resisting this pull by remembering who we are and where we are headed.

WEEK 1, DAY 1

Absorb 1 Peter 1:1–12 by reading it aloud several times until you become familiar with its verses, words, and phrases.

WEEK 1, DAY 2

1 PETER 1:1-12

The Setting

We immediately find ourselves in a letter from one person to another. When we read mail from someone we have never met, we look for clues within the text. As you read the opening verses of 1 Peter, try to detect the character of the writer as well as that of the original readers. The proper position for studying this text is to imagine that we are its recipients—this is the word of the Lord to us.

The Message

The primary themes of an epistle are often suggested in the opening greeting; general statements made early in the letter later unfold into larger discussions. Knowing that you are at the beginning of this letter, pay attention to the hints in these words of greeting. Can you detect the issues in the community? Can you sense how they might need to be encouraged?

To discover the message of 1 Peter 1:1–12, let's divide the passage into four sections. **Summarize or paraphrase the general message or theme of each grouping of verses (following the pattern provided for verses 3–5 and 6–9).**

1. 1 Peter 1:1–2

_____

_____

_____

_____

_____

_____

_____

_____

_____

_____

_____

_____

_____

2. 1 Peter 1:3–5

The author pronounces a prayer of blessing upon the readers. This prayer notes both their past and their future and declares their birthright as children begotten of a heavenly Father. As God's people, they have a Father who has secured an inheritance for them.

3. 1 Peter 1:6–9

The author tells the believers that getting to their inheritance will involve suffering and trials to test the genuineness of their faith. Their hope as sufferers is their faith in Jesus, who is their ultimate salvation.

4. 1 Peter 1:10–12

WEEK 1, DAY 3

What's Happening in the Passage?

As we notice certain circumstances in the story, we will begin to see how they are similar to or different from the realities of our world. The story will become the lens through which we see the world in which we live today. In our study today, you may encounter words and/or phrases that are unfamiliar to you. Some of the particular words and translation choices for them have been explained in more detail in the **Word Study Notes**. If you are interested in even more help or detail, you can supplement this study with a Bible dictionary or other Bible study resource.

Jot down a summary description of the world and reality that is portrayed in the following verses. Follow the pattern provided for 1 Peter 1:3–5 and 1:10–12.

WORD STUDY NOTES #1

[1] The typical structure of ancient letters is evident in this opening address and prayer of blessing.

[2] This opening gives us geographical context which also serves as a metaphor to help us understand the readers as exiles. Additionally, the opening describes the story within which this letter fits—the Trinitarian story of God the Father, Son, and Holy Spirit.

1. 1 Peter 1:1–2[1, 2]

_____

_____

_____

_____

_____

_____

_____

_____

_____

_____

_____

_____

_____

_____

_____

_____

2. 1 Peter 1:3-5

The opening prayer of blessing denotes a timeline that reminds us that, as exiles, we are time travelers; we are moving from a past, toward a future, through the present. The author writes that the readers have been begotten by God (past action), are currently suffering various trials that test them (present action), and are moving toward an inheritance full of glory (future action). Now that they have been born into God's family, their new status gives them hope for a future inheritance. When Christ returns, they will receive this inheritance, which is a living hope.[1] Whether they receive it depends upon their conduct, the identity they embrace, and their faithfulness to the one who birthed them into this living hope. The author assures them that their inheritance is secure. Even death cannot forfeit it, because the Father raised Jesus from the dead into a glorious inheritance. Additionally, their inheritance cannot be stolen, because it is kept in heaven, far from the powers that threaten them on earth.[2]

3. 1 Peter 1:6-9

_____

_____

_____

_____

_____

_____

_____

4. 1 Peter 1:10-12

The author gives a historic perspective on the believers' inheritance, describing it as "the grace that was to come to you" (1:10). The prophets carefully inquired into this grace (1:10), and the Spirit of Christ within them revealed that through suffering, Christ would lead them to it (1:11). One of the consistent reminders in 1 Peter is that the exiles' fate is linked to Jesus's fate. Thus, just as Jesus's suffering led to resurrection and glory, so will theirs. This is the good news that has come from the Father, to the prophets, through the Spirit of Jesus, by way of resurrection, to the exiles.

WORD STUDY NOTES #2

[1] "Living hope" could mean that the death that usually triggers inheritance proceedings has not occurred. Or it could mean that this inheritance is alive with promise and possibility in this given moment.

[2] The author's description of the inheritance reveals that it cannot be embezzled; cannot depreciate; cannot be contested; and cannot be changed or pilfered, because God keeps it secure.

Discoveries

Let's summarize our discoveries from 1 Peter 1:1–12.

1. Our salvation did not begin with our own decision. God was active in our past, even before we were aware of his saving intent.

2. Christianity is more like a journey we are on than a belief system to which we adhere — faith involves traveling.

3. Jesus is our model for faithfulness, our example in suffering, the essence of our inheritance, and the guarantor of our tomorrow. The inheritance of Jesus, as seen in his resurrection from the dead and ascension into heaven, points to our own future inheritance.

4. We cannot guard our own inheritance. The only security we have is in God's keeping power.

WEEK 1, DAY 4

Joy in Suffering and the Story of God

Whenever we read a biblical text, it is important to ask how the particular text we're reading relates to the rest of the Bible. One of the primary themes of 1 Peter is suffering. Even in this opening prayer of blessing, we read that "for a little while you may have had to suffer grief in all kinds of trials" (1 Peter 1:6). The fact that the opening also references Jesus's suffering reminds us that it is impossible to tell the story of God without including suffering as a key component. Strange as it may seem, we often find that joy is the companion of suffering. In most narratives, these two are polar opposites, but in the Christian journey, one leads to the other. **In the space given below, summarize how each passage utilizes the theme of joy in suffering.**

1. Psalm 30

_____

_____

_____

_____

_____

_____

_____

2. Psalm 139:7–12

_____

_____

_____

_____

_____

_____

_____

_____

If you have a study Bible, it may have references in a margin, a middle column, or footnotes that point to other biblical texts. You may find it helpful in understanding how the whole story of God ties together to look up some of those other scriptures from time to time.

19

3. John 15:18–25; 16:16–24; 17:1–26

_____

_____

_____

_____

_____

_____

_____

_____

4. 1 Corinthians 3:10–17

_____

_____

_____

_____

_____

_____

_____

_____

5. 2 Corinthians 1:5–7

_____

_____

_____

_____

_____

_____

_____

_____

6. Philippians 3:10–11

_____

_____

_____

_____

_____

_____

_____

_____

_____

_____

_____

_____

_____

7. Colossians 1:24

_____

_____

_____

_____

_____

_____

_____

_____

_____

_____

_____

_____

_____

_____

_____

_____

WEEK 1, DAY 5

1 Peter and Our World Today

When we look at the theme of our future inheritance in 1 Peter 1:1–12, it can become the lens through which we see ourselves, our world, and how God works in our world today.

1. As Christians, why is it a mistake to think that our inheritance solely entails escaping this world and getting to heaven?

Revelation 21 tells us that the holy city, the New Jerusalem, will come down from heaven. God

will make everything new, including a new heaven and a new earth, and will dwell with us

here. We are not called to escape from a sinful, corrupt earth to a celestial city above-rather,

Christ invites us to journey into the fullness of the kingdom of God.

Following the above example, answer these questions about how we can understand ourselves, our world, and God's action in our world today.

2. Why is the metaphor of an inheritance useful in addressing the exiles?

3. According to 2 Peter, what is the exiles' present responsibility if they wish to receive a future inheritance?

_____

_____

_____

_____

_____

_____

_____

_____

_____

_____

_____

_____

_____

4. What do you believe you will inherit from God?

_____

_____

_____

_____

_____

_____

_____

_____

_____

_____

_____

_____

_____

_____

Invitation and Response

God's Word always invites a response. Think about the way the theme of our future inheritance speaks to us today. How does it invite us to respond?

_____

_____

_____

_____

_____

_____

_____

_____

_____

_____

_____

_____

What is your evaluation of yourself based on any or all of the verses found in 1 Peter 1:1–12?

_____

_____

_____

_____

_____

_____

_____

_____

_____

_____

_____

_____

Christianity is more like a journey we are on than a belief system to which we adhere—faith involves traveling.

1 PETER 1:13-2:10

Defection is common in exile. Removed from the support of family and friends, surrounded by foreign cultural influences, it is easy to forget who we are and look to the opinionated majority for our identity. Our obedience to God places us squarely in culture's crosshairs and invites unwanted attention and scorn.

For this reason, the epistle's opening body masterfully reminds the exiles of their identity: They are the elect household of God; obedient children; a family with a new Father; siblings in a brotherhood; newborn babies; living stones being built into a spiritual house. They are a chosen race, a royal priesthood, a holy nation — they are God's own people. As we see, this may be the densest collection of identifiers in all of Scripture — Peter goes overboard in reminding his readers of their identity. This is because we do not defect when we truly understand and embrace who we are.

WEEK 2, DAY 1

Absorb 1 Peter 1:13–2:10 by reading it aloud several times until you become familiar with its verses, words, and phrases.

WEEK 2, DAY 2

1 PETER 1:13–2:10

The Setting

As with many addresses, the writer begins by reminding the readers of their identity. It is always better to challenge people to be who they are rather than become someone they are not. Without a home or familial practices to reinforce their identity, the readers need a strong reminder of who they are. In this way, Peter offers self-esteem to these exiled eschatological travelers.

The Message

This passage reveals the readers' identity: "Be holy, because I am holy." This quotation in verse 16 comes from the priestly Holiness Code of Leviticus 17–26. In 2:5, the author builds upon this by telling readers they are being formed into a holy priesthood; and again, in 2:9, the writer calls them a royal priesthood. It is clear that the family business is priestly business, and their calling is holiness. We see more instances of priestly language throughout this passage, including "redeemed . . . with the precious blood of . . . a lamb without blemish or defect;" "purified;" and "offering spiritual sacrifices acceptable to God" (1:18–19; 1:22; 2:5).

To discover the message of 1 Peter 1:13–2:10, let's divide the passage into six sections. **Summarize or paraphrase the general message or theme of each grouping of verses (following the pattern provided for 1 Peter 1:13–16 and 2:1–3).**

1. 1 Peter 1:13–16

Now that they have come to faith, the believers must practice mental and behavioral discipline that will reflect readiness for Christ's return. The author reminds the believers that they are not who they used to be. Once, they blindly served their desires in in ignorance without understanding where those desires were leading them. Now they are to live holy lives. The model for this holiness is the holiness of God.

2. 1 Peter 1:17–21

3. 1 Peter 1:22–25

_____
_____
_____
_____
_____
_____
_____
_____
_____

4. 1 Peter 2:1–3

Malice, guile, insincerity, envy, and slander are spiritually withering, but God's Word is
like pure spiritual milk that enables believers to grow. Like a baby desiring its mother's
milk and tasting that it is good, the new believer must drink the milk of God's Word
in order to mature in love.

5. 1 Peter 2:4–8

_____
_____
_____
_____
_____
_____
_____

6. 1 Peter 2:9-10

_____
_____
_____
_____
_____
_____
_____
_____

WEEK 2, DAY 3

What's Happening in the Passage?

As we notice certain circumstances in the story, we will begin to see how they are similar to or different from the realities of our world. The story will become the lens through which we see the world in which we live today. In our study today, you may encounter words and/or phrases that are unfamiliar to you. Some of the particular words and translation choices for them have been explained in more detail in the **Word Study Notes**. If you are interested in even more help or detail, you can supplement this study with a Bible dictionary or other Bible study resource.

Jot down a summary description of the world and reality that is portrayed in the following verses. Follow the pattern provided for 1 Peter 2:4–8 and 2:9–10.

1. 1 Peter 1:13–16

_____

_____

_____

_____

_____

_____

_____

WORD STUDY NOTES #2

[1] The Old Testament atonement sacrifice required a lamb without blemish or defect.

2. 1 Peter 1:17–21[1]

_____

_____

_____

_____

_____

_____

_____

_____

3. 1 Peter 1:22–25

_____

_____

_____

_____

_____

_____

_____

_____

_____

_____

_____

_____

_____

_____

4. 1 Peter 2:1–3

_____

_____

_____

_____

_____

_____

_____

_____

_____

_____

_____

_____

_____

_____

5. 1 Peter 2:4-8

God gave the Holiness Code of Leviticus to Aaron and his sons and, through them, to all the people of Israel. In doing so, God was creating a family of priests who would serve him by mediating his grace to all people on earth. God chose Israel for a purpose. It is important to remember that divine election is not an act of favoritism or exclusion but an act of mission. There was nothing in Israel that merited their chosenness; rather, like a temple, God was building living stones into a spiritual household for the purpose of holy service to him. When Peter addresses the communities of the exile in this way, he is connecting them to the mission of Israel, then to the mission of Jesus. His message is not about the reestablishment of the Jewish temple and sacrificial system—it is about the continuation of God's redemption through the church. The church, like God's priestly Old Testament people, practices an ethical existence in continuity with what God has always required. The call to holiness has not changed; it is still the family business.

6. 1 Peter 2:9-10

Holiness language might remind us of the Pharisees. These religious leaders sought to maintain holiness among God's people, but their efforts created a purity system that became almost impossible to uphold. The Pharisees created strict boundaries that determined what was clean and unclean, pure and impure, holy and profane. This system excluded many people for reasons beyond their control, including gender, occupation, disease, disability, or poverty. Jesus challenged this purity system.[1] The holiness Peter calls for is not a system of gaining access to God by performance. Rather, it is godly behavior; it is Christlikeness. Being part of God's family is not about wielding privilege or finding ways to exclude others; it is about holiness.

Discoveries

Let's summarize our discoveries from 1 Peter 1:13–2:10.

1. Following our desires wherever they lead is an exercise in ignorance.

2. The call to holiness is not an impossible moral commandment but rather the pathway toward what our Creator intended us to be. It is a return to our creational purpose as humans.

3. Our redemption is not rooted in temporary things but in Christ's sacrifice, understood from the foundation of the world. God's imperishable Word reminds us that God has acted to save us.

4. We express belonging to God's family by loving each other deeply, from the heart.

5. As Christians, we live out our faith in stages. We are all infants who need spiritual nourishment as we grow up into a priestly family.

6. The Christian faith is not a solo sport but an exercise in being formed together into a holy community.

Living Stones and the Story of God

Whenever we read a biblical text, it is important to ask how the particular text we're reading relates to the rest of the Bible. The many Old Testament references in this week's passage reveal the author's familiarity with the scope and theology of the ancient texts. **In the space given below, summarize how each passage utilizes the theme of God building his people into a holy household.**

1. Leviticus 17–26

_____

_____

_____

_____

_____

_____

_____

2. Psalm 118

_____

_____

_____

_____

_____

_____

_____

_____

If you have a study Bible, it may have references in a margin, a middle column, or footnotes that point to other biblical texts. You may find it helpful in understanding how the whole story of God ties together to look up some of those other scriptures from time to time.

3. Isaiah 8:14

_____
_____
_____
_____
_____
_____
_____
_____

4. Isaiah 28:16

_____
_____
_____
_____
_____
_____
_____

5. Isaiah 40:6–10

_____
_____
_____
_____
_____
_____
_____
_____

6. Matthew 6:25–34

_____
_____
_____
_____
_____
_____
_____
_____
_____
_____
_____
_____
_____
_____
_____

7. Hebrews 5:11–14

_____
_____
_____
_____
_____
_____
_____
_____
_____
_____
_____
_____
_____
_____
_____

WEEK 2, DAY 5

1 Peter and Our World Today

When we look at the theme of God forming his people into a holy household in 1 Peter 1:13–2:10, it can become the lens through which we see ourselves, our world, and how God works in our world today.

1. In what ways do we see people defect from fully participating in the family of God, even while they are still attending church?

Some churchgoers defect in their devotion and settle for half-hearted compliance rather than

vibrant obedience. Others defect due to generational differences: they don't like the music, the

volume of worship, the way other people in the church are dressed. Still others defect by

withholding their tithe, their attendance, or their willingness to serve.

Following the above example, answer these questions about how we can understand ourselves, our world, and God's action in our world today.

2. What comes to mind when you hear the word "holiness"?

3. In what ways does your understanding of your identity shape your behavior?

_____

_____

_____

_____

_____

_____

_____

_____

_____

_____

_____

4. Of all the family identifiers used in this text, which is most encouraging to you? Why?

_____

_____

_____

_____

_____

_____

_____

_____

_____

_____

_____

_____

_____

5. What happens at the family dinner table that is similar to what happens at the church Communion table?

_____

_____

_____

_____

_____

_____

_____

_____

_____

_____

_____

_____

6. When have you experienced a deep craving for God like a newborn's hunger for its mother's milk? What steps can you take to sustain that desire?

_____

_____

_____

_____

_____

_____

_____

_____

_____

_____

_____

_____

_____

Invitation and Response

God's Word always invites a response. Think about the way the theme of God building his people into a holy household speaks to us today. How does it invite us to respond?

_____

_____

_____

_____

_____

_____

_____

_____

_____

_____

_____

What is your evaluation of yourself based on any or all of the verses found in 1 Peter 1:13–2:10?

_____

_____

_____

_____

_____

_____

_____

_____

_____

_____

_____

The call to holiness is a return to our creational purpose as humans.

1 PETER 2:11–3:12

When studying a text, it is important to recognize the social context of its original audience. A person's standing in the pecking order of society makes a huge difference in how they understand instructions from a spiritual leader. In the case of 1 Peter, the readers are foreigners, outsiders in their city. In exile, people are pushed to the fringes and dismissed as irrelevant. To their neighbors, the believers were "those strange people who don't fit in; those resident foreigners; those folk with odd ways." This marginalization shapes the way they receive the words of 1 Peter.

In this week's passage, we see that our freedom in Christ implies communal responsibility. Our freedom means respecting the rights of all people rather than fighting tooth-and-nail to get our way. It calls for granting others their freedom. Obviously, this call is diametrically opposed to the current culture war championed by many modern-day Christians.

Peter emphasizes that the believers must do good, respect authority, and contribute to society. This echoes how, in the Old Testament Babylonian exile, the prophet instructed God's people to settle down, build homes, and seek the welfare of the city.

Thus, the author calls the believers to live exemplary lives that will discredit the accusations of those who marginalize them. In doing so, the author is also suggesting a way to be welcomed by the local rulers. While this may seem like compromise, it actually reflects Jesus's example, in which, by submitting to the ruling powers, he offered the world a radically different understanding of power.

WEEK 3, DAY 1

Absorb 1 Peter 2:11–3:12 by reading it aloud several times until you become familiar with its verses, words, and phrases.

WEEK 3, DAY 2

1 PETER 2:11–3:12

The Setting

The letter identifies the readers as foreigners and exiles. Taken together, these words describe people who are living as permanent visitors in a place. The culture of Asia Minor allowed for this if the person was there under the favor of a person of status and honor. In these cases, the visitor's presence was conditioned upon the favor of their host. The author assumes that the readers need such favor—thus, they are under some level of scrutiny.

Other comments in 1 Peter suggest that the believers were being maligned and accused of behavior unbecoming a citizen. If they could not refute such claims, their host would be shamed by their presence, and they would be required to honor him by leaving. Peter, seeking to keep the believers in place, encourages exemplary behavior that will make all accusations against them null and void. They are to live such exemplary lives that they bring honor to their host, who will then defend their right to remain in the community.

The Message

When we consider the context of 1 Peter, we can read between the lines and hear the author suggesting that Christians who behave as instructed in the letter will become exemplary citizens. Their kindness, justice, and compassion will make their neighbors glad for their presence. The author applies this instruction to the relationship between slaves and their masters (2:18–21), wives and their husbands (3:1–6), husbands and their wives (3:7), and finally, to relationships in general (3:8–9). In all of these relationships, serving by submission follows Jesus's example as described in 2:21–25.

To discover the message of 1 Peter 2:11–3:12, let's divide the passage into four sections. **Summarize or paraphrase the general message or theme of each grouping of verses (following the pattern provided for 1 Peter 3:8–12).**

1. 1 Peter 2:11–17

_____

_____

_____

_____

2. 1 Peter 2:18–25

_____

_____

_____

_____

_____

_____

_____

_____

_____

_____

3. 1 Peter 3:1–7

_____

_____

_____

_____

_____

_____

_____

_____

_____

_____

_____

4. 1 Peter 3:8–12

In all of our relationships, we are called to demonstrate the hallmarks of God's people. Our unity, sympathy, love, tender hearts, and humble minds will mark us as the people of Jesus. The passage closes with a blessing for those who obey its directives to speak truth, resist evil, do good, and seek peace. The Lord sees these people and answers their prayers. Conversely, the Lord sets his face against those who do evil.

WEEK 3, DAY 3

What's Happening in the Passage?

As we notice certain circumstances in the story, we will begin to see how they are similar to or different from the realities of our world. The story will become the lens through which we see the world in which we live today. In our study today, you may encounter words and/or phrases that are unfamiliar to you. Some of the particular words and translation choices for them have been explained in more detail in the **Word Study Notes**. If you are interested in even more help or detail, you can supplement this study with a Bible dictionary or other Bible study resource.

Jot down a summary description of the world and reality that is portrayed in the following verses. Follow the pattern provided for 1 Peter 2:11–17.

WORD STUDY NOTES #1

[1] The command to live honorably is issued within the context of a culture built around the two poles of shame and honor. In the readers' culture, the behavior of the lower social class brought either shame or honor upon the higher-status people to whom they were accountable.

[2] "Free people" denotes a classification in Roman society that came with certain rights and privileges. We see this dynamic at play when, on occasion, Paul invokes his citizenship with his persecutors, demanding that they respect his legal rights (Acts 22:25). This civic understanding was part of the culture of Asia Minor.

1. 1 Peter 2:11–17

We hear the tension in this instruction: the very people who want to gain the favor of their host benefactors and the civil authorities are called to separate themselves from common cultic practices. Throughout church history, Christians have abstained from some cultural practices as an expression of conformity to Jesus. The question raised here is whether the way we practice abstinence brings shame upon those who rule the culture in which we live.[1,2] This idea may be unfamiliar to Christians who need no approval to live and work where they please. However, an undocumented immigrant might read this text differently. Those who have less freedom of choice rely on acceptance by those who have the power to expel them or cut off their livelihood. This is what it means to be an exile. In the instructions to submit to human authority, the key phrase is "for the Lord's sake" (2:13). It makes sense to obey those with institutional power to save our own skin—but here, the apostle calls us to do so to honor the Lord.

2. 1 Peter 2:18–25[1,2]

_____

_____

_____

_____

_____

_____

_____

_____

3. 1 Peter 3:1–7[1]

_____

_____

_____

_____

_____

_____

_____

_____

4. 1 Peter 3:8–12

_____

_____

_____

_____

_____

_____

_____

_____

_____

WORD STUDY NOTES #2

[1] Verse 22 alludes to a figure described in Isaiah 40–55—the suffering servant of God. This figure could represent the people of Israel, a specific prophet, or one of the messianic kings. However, the identity of the suffering servant is not as important as the role he fulfills. In the New Testament, Jesus assumes the mission of this servant, and the church understands him in this light.

[2] Any use of this text to support the institution of slavery or the domination of women in marriage royally misses the point. Such interpretations contradict the biblical concept of freedom. The discussion of slavery and marriage in Asia Minor is rooted in a time and place far removed from our own. This word from the Lord is not about our right to demand but about our freedom to submit.

WORD STUDY NOTES #3

[1] It is important to read this passage about the wife/husband relationship with an understanding of the cultural context of Asia Minor, in which women had few (if any) rights and were viewed as property. This lack of rights in public life is why the author refers to the wife as "the weaker partner" (3:7).

Discoveries

Let's summarize our discoveries from 1 Peter 2:11–3:12.

1. Christian freedom is never an excuse for doing as we please; rather, it enables us to do as God pleases, regardless of the cost.

2. The witness of a Christian must always be accompanied by honorable deeds.

3. Suffering for doing wrong or for not getting our way does not reflect the suffering of Jesus.

4. The instruction to submit to governing authorities is not a prescriptive, one-size-fits-all command for Christians today. Rather, it describes how the original readers of 1 Peter could best bear witness to Jesus in their social context.

5. We are called to be a people who live under divine blessing and offer that same blessing to others.

6. Believers should be characterized by unity, sympathy, love, tender hearts, and humble minds.

WEEK 3, DAY 4

The Suffering Servant and the Story of God

Whenever we read a biblical text, it is important to ask how the particular text we're reading relates to the rest of the Bible. Jesus's designation as the suffering servant of God is a rich theme in the Christiaon story. **In the space given below, summarize how each passage utilizes the theme of the suffering servant.**

1. Isaiah 42:1–9

_____

_____

_____

_____

_____

_____

_____

_____

2. Isaiah 49:1–7

_____

_____

_____

_____

_____

_____

_____

_____

_____

If you have a study Bible, it may have references in a margin, a middle column, or footnotes that point to other biblical texts. You may find it helpful in understanding how the whole story of God ties together to look up some of those other scriptures from time to time.

3. Isaiah 50:4–11

_____
_____
_____
_____
_____
_____
_____
_____
_____
_____
_____
_____
_____
_____
_____

4. Isaiah 52:13–53:12

_____
_____
_____
_____
_____
_____
_____
_____
_____
_____
_____
_____
_____
_____
_____

5. Luke 4:16–21

6. John 1:29-34

WEEK 3, DAY 5

1 Peter and Our World Today

When we look at the theme of living exemplary lives as exiles in 1 Peter 2:11–3:12, it can become the lens through which we see ourselves, our world, and how God works in our world today.

1. As exiles, how should we approach our everyday work?

Our world revolves around goods and services, production and livelihood. When we perform

our work as a sacred vocation and show up at work every day in a way that improves our

community, we can move out of the margins and into the center of public life. This is how we

make a difference in our society: by working like God works, laboring faithfully like God labors,

creating, healing, teaching, and serving in the trenches of the daily grind.

Following the above example, answer these questions about how we can understand ourselves, our world, and God's action in our world today.

2. How do we submit to economic and political authorities while still obeying the call to be holy as the Lord is holy?

3. If your coworkers had to characterize your God based on the quality of your work, what would they say?

_____
_____
_____
_____
_____
_____
_____
_____
_____
_____
_____
_____
_____
_____

4. What are some specific steps you can take to be a witness for Christ in your workplace?

_____
_____
_____
_____
_____
_____
_____
_____
_____
_____
_____
_____
_____
_____

Invitation and Response

God's Word always invites a response. Think about the way the theme of living exemplary lives as exiles speaks to us today. How does it invite us to respond?

_____

_____

_____

_____

_____

_____

_____

_____

_____

_____

_____

What is your evaluation of yourself based on any or all of the verses found in 1 Peter 2:11–3:12?

_____

_____

_____

_____

_____

_____

_____

_____

_____

_____

_____

We are called to be
a people who live
under divine blessing
and offer that same
blessing to others.

1 PETER 3:13-4:11

Let's refresh our memory of the context of 1 Peter: The exiles of the dispersion are on a journey from their election as God's people to the day of Christ's return. Their current location is a threatening and dangerous place. As they live in the foreign land of Asia Minor, they are tempted to forget their identity, to assimilate to gentile culture, and to defect from the faith.

Along this journey, the believers endure costly trials. The author encourages them to conduct themselves with holiness, because the Father who called them is holy. He also reframes their suffering as participation in the suffering of Jesus and a vital part of their Christian witness. He promises that if they are faithful, they will share in the Lord's glory and be vindicated for their persecution at the Lord's coming. For the next two weeks, we will walk in the shoes of people who suffer for the cause of Christ. We will discover how this is the way of God and the path to glory.

WEEK 4, DAY 1

Absorb 1 Peter 3:13–4:11 by reading it aloud several times until you become familiar with its verses, words, and phrases.

WEEK 4, DAY 2

1 PETER 3:13–4:11

The Setting

When we are reading epistles, we should keep in mind that a conversation is occurring between the writer and the readers. The writer anticipates the recipients' reactions based on his experiences with them. He can imagine the looks on their faces as they hear the letter read to the church.

Likewise, as we study Scripture, a conversation about the alignment of our lives with biblical revelation is brewing between us and the Spirit of God. These are living letters.

The Message

We concluded the previous section with a prayer of blessing (3:10–12) which reminds us that the Lord's eyes are on the righteous, and he hears their prayers; but he turns his face against those who do evil.

A persecuted believer reading this may well argue, "If God is for us and hears our prayers, why are we being treated as exiles and foreigners? Why are we being attacked and persecuted as followers of God's ways? And if God's face is against those who do evil, why are they getting away with treating us this way?"

To discover the message of 1 Peter 3:13–4:11, let's divide the passage into five sections. **Summarize or paraphrase the general message or theme of each grouping of verses (following the pattern provided for 1 Peter 4:1–6 and 7–11).**

1. 1 Peter 3:13–14

_____

_____

_____

_____

_____

_____

_____

2. 1 Peter 3:15–16

_____

_____

_____

_____

_____

_____

_____

_____

3. 1 Peter 3:17–22

_____

_____

_____

_____

_____

_____

_____

_____

_____

4. 1 Peter 4:1–6

We must arm ourselves with the attitude of Christ as we bear our own suffering. We are to live holy lives, abstaining from the immoral practices of worldly people. While this may surprise them and cause them to curse us, we should leave them in God's hands—they will be accountable to God for their actions.

5. 1 Peter 4:7–11

The closing instructions of this section describe the exemplary lives we are called to live. Our lives must be characterized by alertness, readiness, discipline, prayer, love, hospitality, service, and worship toward God.

WEEK 4, DAY 3

What's Happening in the Passage?

As we notice certain circumstances in the story, we will begin to see how they are similar to or different from the realities of our world. The story will become the lens through which we see the world in which we live today. In our study today, you may encounter words and/or phrases that are unfamiliar to you. Some of the particular words and translation choices for them have been explained in more detail in the **Word Study Notes**. If you are interested in even more help or detail, you can supplement this study with a Bible dictionary or other Bible study resource.

Jot down a summary description of the world and reality that is portrayed in the following verses. Follow the pattern provided for 1 Peter 3:13–14 and 17–22.

WORD STUDY NOTES #1

[1]Jesus said, "Blessed are those who are persecuted because of righteousness, for theirs is the kingdom of heaven. Blessed are you when people insult you, persecute you and falsely say all kinds of evil against you because of me. Rejoice and be glad, because great is your reward in heaven" (Matthew 5:10-12a).

1. 1 Peter 3:13–14

The author launches into a hypothetical scenario in which believers might suffer for doing what is right: "Who will harm you if you are eager to do good?" Rather than answer the question, the author declares that when we suffer for doing what is right, we are blessed. Echoes of the Sermon on the Mount ring in our ears.[1]

2. 1 Peter 3:15–16

_____

_____

_____

_____

_____

_____

_____

_____

3. 1 Peter 3:17–22

Verse 18 is the hinge in the text. We shift from instructions on how to suffer to considering Christ as the example of why we willingly suffer for doing good. Jesus suffered for the salvation of the unrighteous. An illustration from the story of Noah follows. Evil was rampant in Noah's day, and people were confident that God could not topple them. God waited patiently in hopes of saving more people, but ultimately, evil had to be confronted, and in order to save the human race, God judged the world with a devastating flood.[1] After this judgment, there was a "resurrection" in the salvation of the eight people who were on the ark. They were saved as witnesses of God's saving intent. Just as humankind was saved by the ark, we too are saved by Jesus's resurrection.

4. 1 Peter 4:1–6

_____

_____

_____

_____

_____

_____

_____

5. 1 Peter 4:7–11

_____

_____

_____

_____

_____

_____

_____

_____

_____

WORD STUDY NOTES #3

[1] Verse 19 says that Jesus, when he was crucified, went to the grave and made a proclamation to the dead, particularly to those who disobeyed God during the days of Noah and perished in the flood. In the context of 1 Peter, it seems that the believers were asking about the fate of those who died before hearing the good news of the gospel. As the author instructs believers who are suffering for their faith, he also addresses this question. While the reference to Jesus's proclamation is mysterious, it illustrates that for both the sufferer and the departed, there is wideness in God's rich mercy. And while these are scant references to build a robust theology on, this kind of mercy seems in keeping with the God who calls all to repentance.

Discoveries

Let's summarize our discoveries from 1 Peter 3:13–4:11.

1. Christians have always wished for a world in which doing good to others was rewarded.

2. One of the most paradoxical teachings of our faith is that we are blessed when we are persecuted for Christ's sake.

3. Though God's ways are often strange to us, they are always saving.

4. Fear of others hinders our ability to faithfully witness. Only Christ in our hearts can deliver us from this fear.

WEEK 4, DAY 4

Suffering, Salvation, and the Story of God

Whenever we read a biblical text, it is important to ask how the particular text we're reading relates to the rest of the Bible. As this week's passage makes clear, our suffering for doing good is connected to God's mission to redeem the world. The text describes the great lengths to which God will go to save a recalcitrant and rebellious people. We see that the larger story of Scripture is God's intent to redeem all of creation. **In the space given below, summarize how each passage utilizes the themes of God's saving intent and bearing witness in the face of opposition.**

1. Acts 4:1–37

_____

_____

_____

_____

_____

_____

_____

_____

2. Acts 14:8–28

_____

_____

_____

_____

_____

_____

_____

_____

_____

_____

If you have a study Bible, it may have references in a margin, a middle column, or footnotes that point to other biblical texts. You may find it helpful in understanding how the whole story of God ties together to look up some of those other scriptures from time to time.

3. Romans 1:16–17

_____

_____

_____

_____

_____

_____

_____

_____

_____

4. Colossians 1:24–29

_____

_____

_____

_____

_____

_____

_____

_____

_____

5. Revelation 11

_____

_____

_____

_____

_____

_____

_____

_____

_____

WEEK 4, DAY 5

1 Peter and Our World Today

When we look at the theme of suffering for the sake of Christ in 1 Peter 3:13–4:11, it can become the lens through which we see ourselves, our world, and how God works in our world today.

1. Why would others curse us for refusing to participate in immorality, as 1 Peter 4:3–4 suggests?

Holiness is at odds with human nature. For this reason, when we abstain from sinful practices

and behaviors, we are sure to make people around us feel jarred, baffled, frustrated, or

convicted. People lash out against what they do not understand.

Following the above example, answer these questions about how we can understand ourselves, our world, and God's action in our world today.

2. Some people claim that suffering detracts from our witness because it prevents us from demonstrating God's victory over evil. How would you respond to this argument?

3. Think about a current or recent trial in your life. If someone asked you to "give the reason for the hope that you have" (3:15), what would you say?

_____

_____

_____

_____

_____

_____

_____

_____

_____

_____

_____

_____

4. What do we mean when we say, "The blood of the martyrs is the seed of the church"?

_____

_____

_____

_____

_____

_____

_____

_____

_____

_____

_____

_____

_____

_____

_____

Invitation and Response

God's Word always invites a response. Think about the way the theme of suffering for the sake of Christ speaks to us today. How does it invite us to respond?

_____

_____

_____

_____

_____

_____

_____

_____

_____

_____

_____

What is your evaluation of yourself based on any or all of the verses found in 1 Peter 3:13–4:11?

_____

_____

_____

_____

_____

_____

_____

_____

_____

_____

_____

One of the most par-
adoxical teachings
of our faith is that
we are blessed when
we are persecuted
for Christ's sake.

1 PETER 4:12–5:11

When we are in exile, we have little cultural or political power. Sometimes we once had it and have now lost it, as in the Babylonian exile. Sometimes, we never had it to begin with, like the church of 1 Peter. And we feel oppressed.

In Isaiah's Babylon, God's people were force-marched five hundred miles from their sacred Jerusalem to a place they did not want to be. They went to bed one night in Jerusalem with their Jewish temple, laws, holidays, songs, king, army, walls, and texts. Then they woke up in exile to gods with strange names, songs they'd never heard, languages they didn't know, and a culture that felt foreign. They wanted to go home, back to yesteryear. They begged God to take them back, to make them great again. And God said no. Instead, he told them, "It is too small a thing for you to be my servant to restore the tribes of Jacob and bring back those of Israel I have kept. I will also make you a light for the Gentiles, that my salvation may reach to the ends of the earth" (Isaiah 49:6). God's plans for our future do not involve taking us back to yesteryear when we were in charge.

The New Testament community experienced much of the same—reading between the lines, they were taking it on the chin from the dark powers that ran their world. However, the author of 1 Peter says that the antidote to their suffering is not escape but joy in the knowledge that they are sharing in Christ's suffering.

WEEK 5, DAY 1

Absorb 1 Peter 4:12–5:11 by reading it aloud several times until you become familiar with its verses, words, and phrases.

WEEK 5, DAY 2

1 PETER 4:12–5:11

The Setting

In 1 Peter 3:13–4:11, the author addresses suffering theoretically. The discussion revolves around suffering for doing good. Rather than answering the "Why us?" question, the author addresses the meaning behind suffering, describing it as the means by which God saves his creatures. From Noah to Jesus, suffering and death were the prelude to resurrection. This gives the people of Asia Minor a rationale for their suffering.

The Message

As we move into this section of the text, the language changes from describing theoretical suffering to describing real suffering. The author addresses the readers' response to the trials they are undergoing in two ways: First, he connects their suffering to Christ's suffering. Second, he suggests that as they comprehend their missional connection with Christ, they will rejoice. The idea of rejoicing in suffering is the key theme of these verses.

To discover the message of 1 Peter 4:12–5:11, let's divide the passage into seven sections. **Summarize or paraphrase the general message or theme of each grouping of verses (following the pattern provided for 1 Peter 4:12–13 and 14–16).**

1. 1 Peter 4:12–13

The section begins with a note that normalizes suffering. When we expect trials as a normal part of our Christian journey, we are not surprised by them. This experience connects us to Jesus, his mission, and his glory.

2. 1 Peter 4:14–16

When we are reviled for Christ's name, we are blessed, and the spirit of glory, which is the Spirit of God, rests on us. However, suffering that arises from doing wrong does not bring blessing or glory. A Christian should never think that the consequences of doing evil connect us to Christ's suffering—just the opposite. We are called to rejoice when we suffer for righteousness.

3. 1 Peter 4:17–19

_____

_____

_____

_____

_____

_____

_____

4. 1 Peter 5:1–4

_____

_____

_____

_____

_____

_____

_____

_____

5. 1 Peter 5:5–7

_____

_____

_____

_____

_____

_____

_____

_____

6. 1 Peter 5:8–9

_____

_____

_____

_____

_____

_____

_____

_____

_____

_____

_____

_____

7. 1 Peter 5:10–11

_____

_____

_____

_____

_____

_____

_____

_____

_____

_____

_____

_____

_____

WEEK 5, DAY 3

What's Happening in the Passage?

As we notice certain circumstances in the story, we will begin to see how they are similar to or different from the realities of our world. The story will become the lens through which we see the world in which we live today. In our study today, you may encounter words and/or phrases that are unfamiliar to you. Some of the particular words and translation choices for them have been explained in more detail in the **Word Study Notes**. If you are interested in even more help or detail, you can supplement this study with a Bible dictionary or other Bible study resource.

Jot down a summary description of the world and reality that is portrayed in the following verses. Follow the pattern provided for 1 Peter 5:1–4, 5–7, and 10–11.

1. 1 Peter 4:12–13

_____

_____

_____

_____

_____

_____

_____

_____

_____

2. 1 Peter 4:14–16

_____

_____

_____

_____

_____

_____

_____

_____

_____

3. 1 Peter 4:17–19

_____
_____
_____
_____
_____
_____
_____
_____
_____
_____
_____
_____
_____
_____
_____
_____
_____
_____
_____
_____
_____
_____
_____

4. 1 Peter 5:1–4

The tone shifts in 5:1 as the author's pastoral heart begins to emerge.[1] He gives the elders instructions for leading God's people.

5. 1 Peter 5:5–7

The author addresses younger people, and then provides instructions for everyone. He instructs the young men to accept the elders.[1]

WORD STUDY NOTES #4

[1] Because of sections like this, 1 Peter is grouped with a set of New Testament letters called the pastoral epistles.

WORD STUDY NOTES #5

[1] The term "elder" is used to identify a leader in the church. It has to do with role more than with age.

6. 1 Peter 5:8–9

_____
_____
_____
_____
_____
_____
_____
_____
_____
_____
_____
_____
_____
_____
_____
_____
_____
_____

7. 1 Peter 5:10–11

The passage closes with a reminder that the believers are not alone and that their trials will not last forever.

Discoveries

Let's summarize our discoveries from 1 Peter 4:12–5:11.

1. It is important to distinguish between suffering that we bring upon ourselves and suffering for Jesus's sake.

2. God has formed the church into a community for our collective benefit.

3. In God's flock, leadership is more about humility and service than power and position.

4. The best thing a shepherd-leader can do is follow the example of Jesus, the great shepherd.

5. There is an evil force in the world called the devil, and he is relentless in his attempts to devour us.

6. We are never alone in our suffering — Christians around the world experience the same thing.

7. God is the only power in the world who can transform suffering into glory.

If you have a study Bible, it may have references in a margin, a middle column, or footnotes that point to other biblical texts. You may find it helpful in understanding how the whole story of God ties together to look up some of those other scriptures from time to time.

Humility and the Story of God

Whenever we read a biblical text, it is important to ask how the particular text we're reading relates to the rest of the Bible. One of the themes in 1 Peter is humility. We see it throughout the book in the instructions to submit to authorities; the example of the suffering Christ; the discussion of slave/master and husband/wife relationships; and the challenge to give account for the hope that is in us. In this week's passage, the author instructs the people thus: "clothe yourselves with humility toward one another, because 'God opposes the proud, but shows favor to the humble'" (5:5). The author then tells the people, "Humble yourselves, therefore, under God's mighty hand" (5:6). Humility is a hallmark of people who live faithfully in exile. **In the space given below, summarize how each passage utilizes the theme of humility.**

1. Proverbs 3:34

_____

_____

_____

_____

_____

_____

2. Daniel 4

_____

_____

_____

_____

_____

_____

_____

3. Luke 1:46–55

_____
_____
_____
_____
_____
_____
_____
_____
_____

4. Luke 6:20–26

_____
_____
_____
_____
_____
_____
_____
_____
_____

5. Luke 14:7–14

_____
_____
_____
_____
_____
_____
_____
_____
_____

6. Philippians 2:5–11

_____
_____
_____
_____
_____
_____
_____
_____
_____
_____
_____
_____
_____
_____

7. James 4:6–10

_____
_____
_____
_____
_____
_____
_____
_____
_____
_____
_____
_____
_____
_____
_____
_____

WEEK 5, DAY 5

1 Peter and Our World Today

When we look at the themes of suffering and humility in 1 Peter 4:12–5:11, they can become the lens through which we see ourselves, our world, and how God works in our world today.

1. According to this week's passage, how should our identity as "eschatological travelers" shape our expectations regarding suffering?

We should not be dismayed or surprised by suffering. Rather, as we journey toward the day when the kingdom of God breaks in upon creation and makes all things new, we should anticipate suffering. Until that day, we should rejoice in our suffering, because it reminds us that we are partners with Jesus and his coming kingdom.

Following the above example, answer these questions about how we can understand ourselves, our world, and God's action in our world today.

2. In light of 1 Peter 4:12–5:11, is it right to say that it is God's will for us to suffer?

3. We may fear that in humbling ourselves, we will invite other people to take advantage of us. How do 1 Peter's teachings about suffering and humility address this fear?

_____

_____

_____

_____

_____

_____

_____

_____

_____

_____

_____

_____

4. Where have you recently seen God opposing the proud and exalting the humble?

_____

_____

_____

_____

_____

_____

_____

_____

_____

_____

_____

_____

Invitation and Response

God's Word always invites a response. Think about the way the themes of suffering and humility speak to us today. How does it invite us to respond?

_____

_____

_____

_____

_____

_____

_____

_____

_____

_____

_____

_____

_____

What is your evaluation of yourself based on any or all of the verses found in 1 Peter 4:12–5:11?

_____

_____

_____

_____

_____

_____

_____

_____

_____

_____

_____

_____

_____

> In God's flock, leadership is
> more about humility and service
> than power and position.

2 PETER 1:1-21

Welcome to 2 Peter. It is a short, sixty-one-verse letter whose writing was prompted by the emergence of false teachers.

Here is the situation: Early Christians believed that Jesus's return was imminent and would occur during their lifetime. As first-generation believers began to die, false teachers began to suggest that the apostles' teaching regarding Jesus's return was incorrect. They called into question not only the doctrine of the parousia (the second coming), but also the apostles' authority as interpreters of the Old Testament. In denying Jesus's return, these false teachers also denied the reality of a coming judgment that would bring moral accountability. By claiming that ethical readiness for the second coming of Christ was unnecessary, they minimized and degraded the call to a holy life. This drove a dagger through the heart of the apostolic teachings about holiness of heart and life.

In our devotional journey this week, we will explore this letter from several vantage points before studying its theological themes.

WEEK 6, DAY 1

Absorb 2 Peter 1:1–21 by reading it aloud several times until you become familiar with its verses, words, and phrases.

WEEK 6, DAY 2

2 PETER 1:1-21

The Setting

The social context of the early Christians addressed in 2 Peter is similar to that of 1 Peter. Like the readers of 1 Peter, they lived in the cities of Asia Minor. The author discourages the believers from participating in the pagan festivals there with their meat sacrificed to gods, sexual immorality, and drunken celebrations. However, belonging to the guilds that sponsored these festivals was the path to socioeconomic success in these cities. Guild membership was also a way of supporting the local manifestation of Roman rule.

These Christians had sacrificed acceptance and wealth as an act of loyalty to Christ, the true King. However, the false teachers' claims offered them an easy out from such costly discipleship. Once their obedience was deemed unnecessary, immature Christians would be ripe for the picking.

The Message

This text bears features of two distinct literary genres: epistle and testament. The marks of an epistle, or letter, are evident in the opening greeting—though it is somewhat different from the one in 1 Peter, it is a customary greeting. After the greeting, the letter bears more resemblance to a testament. Similar to our modern idea of a last will and testament, this ancient literary genre was used to express dying wishes and impart wisdom.

To discover the message of 2 Peter 1:1–21, let's divide the passage into seven sections. **Summarize or paraphrase the general message or theme of each grouping of verses (following the pattern provided for verses 3–4).**

1. 2 Peter 1:1–2

_____

_____

_____

_____

_____

_____

2. 2 Peter 1:3–4

Because he is good, God called us to himself. By revealing himself to us, God has empowered us to break free from the evil in the world and live in a way that glorifies him.

3. 2 Peter 1:5–9

4. 2 Peter 1:10–11

5. 2 Peter 1:12–15

_____

_____

_____

_____

_____

_____

_____

_____

6. 2 Peter 1:16–18

_____

_____

_____

_____

_____

_____

_____

_____

_____

7. 2 Peter 1:19–21

_____

_____

_____

_____

_____

_____

_____

_____

_____

WEEK 6, DAY 3

What's Happening in the Passage?

As we notice certain circumstances in the story, we will begin to see how they are similar to or different from the realities of our world. The story will become the lens through which we see the world in which we live today. In our study today, you may encounter words and/or phrases that are unfamiliar to you. Some of the particular words and translation choices for them have been explained in more detail in the **Word Study Notes**. If you are interested in even more help or detail, you can supplement this study with a Bible dictionary or other Bible study resource.

Jot down a summary description of the world and reality that is portrayed in the following verses. Follow the pattern provided for 2 Peter 1:1–2 and 12–15.

1. 2 Peter 1:1–2

The attribution to Simon Peter roots this letter in the rich theological history of Jesus and the apostles. While most likely written by a follower of Peter, the text uses the connection between Peter and Jesus to lend authority to the letter.

In the letter's opening, we learn what is most essential to the writer: a faith that is precious. He values the faith imparted to the church by the early apostles' teaching. As we have seen, the letter will directly address the false teachers and the erosion of trust in the gospel of Jesus. Verse 2 concludes with a customary prayer of blessing—that grace and peace might be theirs in abundance—but we also get an added note that this abundance flows from the knowledge[1] of the Lord Jesus.

2. 2 Peter 1:3–4

WORD STUDY NOTES #1

[1] The word translated "knowledge" means more than "information about." It is the same word used for the intimacy of marriage—that is, a personal knowledge rooted in shared experience.

_____

_____

_____

_____

_____

3. 2 Peter 1:5–9

_____

_____

_____

_____

_____

_____

_____

_____

_____

_____

4. 2 Peter 1:10–11

_____

_____

_____

_____

_____

_____

_____

_____

_____

5. 2 Peter 1:12–15

The reminders in this text are common to this genre: the beloved apostle has delivered the faith to his readers; the apostle has consistently reminded them of this truth throughout his lifetime; the apostle's impending death calls for one last reminder; and the apostle expects the readers to remember these things after his passing.

6. 2 Peter 1:16–18

---

7. 2 Peter 1:19–21[1]

WORD STUDY NOTES #7

[1] The books of the Bible were admitted to the canon (the accepted collection of the sixty-six books of the Bible) based on several qualifications. One of the qualifications for New Testament books was authorship by a contemporary of Jesus—a follower, apostle, or disciple. These writers were eyewitnesses of the Christ. Another qualification was that the book was already being circulated among and used by the early Christians. With modern linguistic techniques, we are able to determine an author's familiarity with language, ancient scriptures, terminology, and social contexts. The early church councils did not have these advantages. Yet the early church was well aware that the Holy Spirit spoke to early Christians through certain epistles.

Discoveries

Let's summarize some of our discoveries from 2 Peter 1:1–21.

1. Leaders of the church are responsible for imparting and preserving the faith that was given to them.

2. Remembering the truth we've received is a necessary part of the Christian faith. To forget is to lose touch with our roots.

3. God's promises are our hedge against the corruption of the world.

4. The knowledge of God is more than information—it is relational intimacy. We are not called to know *about God* but to *know God*.

5. The Christian life cannot be lived on cruise control. It requires effort, eagerness to confirm our call, and a faithful memory of what has been entrusted to us.

6. The faith we have received comes from eyewitnesses to the events they testify about—our sources are original.

WEEK 6, DAY 4

The Testaments of Scripture and the Story of God

Whenever we read a biblical text, it is important to ask how the particular text we're reading relates to the rest of the Bible. As we saw earlier in the week, the middle section of the letter (1:3–3:13) has some characteristics of a testament. In a testament, a leader announces his imminent death, then reviews ethical teachings and traditions that he wants the community to continue observing after his death. This literary form was popular in Judaism and was used to relate the last words of renowned men in and beyond the Old Testament. Early Christian writers later adopted the genre.

In the space given below, write a short summary of how these testaments function for the people of God. How are they similar to 2 Peter 1? Note what gives weight and authority to these testaments.

1. Genesis 49

_____

_____

_____

_____

_____

_____

2. Deuteronomy 33

_____

_____

_____

_____

_____

_____

_____

If you have a study Bible, it may have references in a margin, a middle column, or footnotes that point to other biblical texts. You may find it helpful in understanding how the whole story of God ties together to look up some of those other scriptures from time to time.

3. John 13–17

_____

_____

_____

_____

_____

_____

_____

_____

4. Acts 20:17–34

_____

_____

_____

_____

_____

_____

_____

_____

5. 2 Timothy

_____

_____

_____

_____

_____

_____

_____

_____

_____

WEEK 6, DAY 5

2 Peter and Our World Today

When we look at the theme of bearing witness to Jesus's majesty in 2 Peter 1:1–21, it can become the lens through which we see ourselves, our world, and how God works in our world today.

1. What is the significance of the reference to Jesus's baptism in 2 Peter 1:17?

The author of 2 Peter describes not only witnessing John's baptism of Jesus, but hearing the

voice from heaven declare, "This is my Son, whom I love; with him I am well pleased" (1:17b).

In attesting to God the Father's blessing upon Jesus, the author authenticates the apostolic

community as witnesses to divine revelation. If the false teachers deny Jesus's promised return,

they must discredit this divine revelation.

Following the above example, answer these questions about how we can understand ourselves, our world, and God's action in our world today.

2. What might motivate false teachers (in both the early church and the modern church) to spread false doctrine?

3. What are the false teachings of today that have potential to create disastrous eternal consequences?

_____

_____

_____

_____

_____

_____

_____

_____

_____

_____

4. If 2 Peter were written to your congregation, what slippery ethical issue would be the primary point of contention?

_____

_____

_____

_____

_____

_____

_____

_____

_____

_____

_____

_____

Invitation and Response

God's Word always invites a response. Reflect on how 2 Peter 1:1–21 prompts you to think about the authenticity of your faith, your personal knowledge of God, and the importance of remembering the faith that has been handed down to you. How does it invite you to respond?

_____

_____

_____

_____

_____

_____

_____

_____

_____

_____

_____

What is your evaluation of yourself based on any or all of the verses found in 2 Peter 1:1–21?

_____

_____

_____

_____

_____

_____

_____

_____

_____

_____

The knowledge of
God is more than
information—it is
relational intimacy.
We are not called
to know about God
but to know God.

2 PETER 2:1-3:18

The book of 2 Peter is limited in its theological scope because it focuses on two primary issues: false teaching regarding Christ's return, and the necessity of ethical behavior. In doing so, it invites us to see an important connection between ethics and Christ's second coming.

One of the primary problems for the church of 2 Peter was participation in pagan feasts. The reference to "lustful desires of the flesh" in 2:18 suggests that the author is particularly concerned with the sexual immorality that came with the cultic feasts.

If Christ's return is a myth, as the false teachers claim, then the coming judgment is also in question. If this is true, what do we do with the injunctions to live holy lives in readiness for Jesus's return? This is not to suggest that the only reason for holiness is a future reward. But if Jesus were never returning, and if we believed that we would never have to account for our deeds, would we still embrace the holy life as an act of devotion to God?

These two chapters are a good wake-up call for a faith that has molded itself around the dominant culture. When there is no discernible difference between the people of God and the pagans of the marketplace, what does it matter that Christ has died, Christ has risen, and Christ will come again? The writer of 2 Peter draws a firm line in the sand and calls the church to holiness in word and deed.

99

WEEK 7, DAY 1

Absorb 2 Peter 2:1–3:18 by reading it aloud several times until you become familiar with its verses, words, and phrases.

WEEK 7, DAY 2

2 PETER 2:1–3:18

The Setting

The opening chapter of 2 Peter discussed the believers' call and election, reminded them of the truth delivered to them by the apostles, and testified eloquently about being an eyewitness to Jesus's majesty.

In chapters 2 and 3, however, the letter's tone changes dramatically. These may be some of the most condemning statements in Scripture. False prophets are called licentious, destructive, greedy, exploitive, hell-bound, chained in deep darkness, slanderous, under divine punishment, irrational animals, born to be caught and killed — and this is only the beginning. We feel the heat of this scorching castigation of those who seek to lead people astray. This is apostolic anger at a fever pitch.

The Message

The message of our text this week moves from condemnation of the false prophets to an attack on their motives and behavior. After this, the writer's tone softens as he assures the believers of Jesus's return, even as he continues to take jabs at the false teachers: he calls them scoffers who indulge their own lusts rather than reflect faithfulness to the ancient prophets. In imagining Jesus's return, we hear the final judgment described as a consuming fire that melts the earth. The closing is a fresh call to holiness and godliness — a call which could be easy to miss given the scorching anger of the majority of the text. Undoubtedly this is why this little book is rarely used in the modern church — but perhaps it contains hidden treasures that we are ignoring.

To discover the message of 2 Peter 2:1–3:18, let's divide the passage into nine sections. **Summarize or paraphrase the general message or theme of each grouping of verses (following the pattern provided for 2 Peter 2:1–3; 3:1–3; 3:4–7; and 3:8–13).**

1. 2 Peter 2:1–3

The writer reminds the believers that false teachers will spread destructive opinions and deny

Christ, and thus bring destruction upon themselves. These heretics will deceive some believers

as they seek to exploit and malign the way of God.

2. 2 Peter 2:4–10a

3. 2 Peter 2:10b–12

4. 2 Peter 2:13–16

5. 2 Peter 2:17–22

_____

_____

_____

_____

_____

6. 2 Peter 3:1–3

The author reminds the readers to heed God's words as imparted by the prophets and the

apostles. False teachers will arise and attempt to lead them astray.

7. 2 Peter 3:4–7

The false teachers claim that, though Jesus promised to come again, things are the same as

they've always been, and time marches on without any proof of his return. The apostle

rebukes this argument and reminds the believers that the Lord will come in judgment. The

same God who created the world and who pronounced judgment in the flood of Noah's day

has reserved the heavens and earth for a coming judgment of fire.

8. 2 Peter 3:8–13

God's sense of time transcends ours. For this reason, the Lord is not slow or overdue in making

his triumphant return; rather, he is being patient so that everyone might have the opportunity

to repent. Therefore, it behooves us to lead lives of holiness and godliness as we wait for this

day of penetrating, purifying judgment by fire that will institute a new heaven and a new earth.

9. 2 Peter 3:14–18

_____

_____

_____

_____

_____

WEEK 7, DAY 3

What's Happening in the Passage?

As we notice certain circumstances in the story, we will begin to see how they are similar to or different from the realities of our world. The story will become the lens through which we see the world in which we live today. In our study today, you may encounter words and/or phrases that are unfamiliar to you. Some of the particular words and translation choices for them have been explained in more detail in the **Word Study Notes**. If you are interested in even more help or detail, you can supplement this study with a Bible dictionary or other Bible study resource.

Jot down a summary description of the world and reality that is portrayed in the following verses. Follow the pattern provided for 2 Peter 2:4–10a.

1. 2 Peter 2:1–3

_____

_____

_____

_____

_____

_____

2. 2 Peter 2:4–10a

WORD STUDY NOTES #2

[1] You may remember that the Noah story is also referenced in 1 Peter 3:18–20. It is the classic example the New Testament employs to illustrate God's capacity to judge sin.

This section of the letter rehearses a litany of Old Testament judgments—it might even be the hall of fame for texts of divine wrath. The author makes back-to-back allusions to the judgment of angels, the flood of Noah's day (Genesis 6–8),[1] and the incineration of Sodom and Gomorrah (Genesis 19). Noah and Lot are the two shining examples of people who lived faithfully in the midst of evil. Noah is called a herald of righteousness; Lot is described as a righteous man who was tormented in his soul by the evil deeds of the people around him. The writer is reminding the readers that they are relatives of Noah and Lot—just as God saved the ancient heroes, God will deliver them too.

3. 2 Peter 2:10b–12

_____

_____

_____

_____

_____

WORD STUDY NOTES #4

[1] The behaviors described in these verses—revelry, sexual sin, and drunkenness—are also associated with the Roman guilds and cults that practiced emperor worship and idol worship.

[2] The story of Balaam and the talking donkey is found in Numbers 22.

4. 2 Peter 2:13–16 [1, 2]

_____

_____

_____

_____

_____

104

5. 2 Peter 2:17–22

_____

_____

_____

_____

_____

6. 2 Peter 3:1–3

_____

_____

_____

_____

_____

7. 2 Peter 3:4–7

8. 2 Peter 3:8–13

9. 2 Peter 3:14–18

Discoveries

Let's summarize our discoveries from 2 Peter 2:1–3:18.

1. God has a proven history of destroying those who destroy others: see the stories of Noah, Lot, and Balaam.

2. Modern deceptions cannot drown out centuries of faithful revelation about Jesus's return. The God who spoke and acted in the past has spoken about the future and will bring it to pass.

3. God's anger is rooted in love; he desires for his creatures to hear the truth and be saved. Any twisting of this godly message is unacceptable and merits divine wrath.

4. God's heart is revealed in the words, "not wanting anyone to perish, but everyone to come to repentance" (2 Peter 3:9b). Divine judgment is connected to this divine intent.

WEEK 7, DAY 4

False Teaching and the Story of God

Whenever we read a biblical text, it is important to ask how the particular text we're reading relates to the rest of the Bible. It is important to allow scripture to interpret scripture. Several commentators have noted the resemblance between the Epistle of Jude and 2 Peter. It may be the case that 2 Peter borrows from Jude, Jude borrows from 2 Peter, or they have a common source from which they both borrow. This is similar to how the Gospels draw on each other and from common sources. Yet the way one author tells the story of Jesus may differ from the way another author tells it. This should not cause us to doubt the authority of Scripture—rather, it should affirm our faith. In the case of the Gospels, multiple witnesses with different perspectives came to the same essential conclusions about Jesus's work and ministry.

The same is true of the Epistles. As the letters were read to different congregations, early Christians began to affirm their faith on the basis of converging evidence from multiple apostles. We often see the same Old Testament references used to make a point or the same arguments used to confront false doctrines. **In the space given below, summarize how each passage utilizes the themes of false teachings and ungodly people.**

1. Matthew 7:15–23

_____

_____

_____

_____

_____

_____

_____

_____

_____

If you have a study Bible, it may have references in a margin, a middle column, or footnotes that point to other biblical texts. You may find it helpful in understanding how the whole story of God ties together to look up some of those other scriptures from time to time.

2. Colossians 2:18–23

_____

_____

_____

_____

_____

_____

_____

_____

_____

3. 1 Timothy 6:3–5

_____

_____

_____

_____

_____

4. Jude 1:4–13

_____

_____

_____

_____

_____

5. Jude 1:16–18

_____

_____

_____

_____

_____

WEEK 7, DAY 5

2 Peter and Our World Today

When we look at the theme of divine judgment in 2 Peter 2:1–3:18, it can become the lens through which we see ourselves, our world, and how God works in our world today.

1. What are the implications of 2 Peter 2:1–3:18 when it comes to weighing the words of teachers and preachers in the church today?

This passage makes it clear that the teachings we live by are a matter of eternal

significance-false teachers bring destruction upon themselves, and those who follow them

will share in their fate. Thus, it is crucial that we carefully weigh our leaders' words against

the testimony of Scripture rather than adopt the teachings of those who offer the easiest path.

Following the above example, answer these questions about how we can understand ourselves, our world, and God's action in our world today.

2. Our passage this week references the flood, the judgment of Sodom and Gomorrah, and other Old Testament narratives. What are some other biblical examples of God enacting divine judgment?

_____

_____

_____

_____

_____

3. Why is it a mistake to think of God's judgment as a solely eschatological (end-of-the-world) event?

_____

_____

_____

_____

_____

4. What is the best way to make the warning of 2 Peter 2:1–3:18 heard today?

_____

_____

_____

_____

_____

_____

_____

_____

_____

_____

_____

5. As you consider 2 Peter 2:1–3:18, does it affect any of your fixed ideas about God and God's character? How so?

_____

_____

_____

_____

_____

_____

_____

_____

_____

_____

_____

_____

_____

_____

Invitation and Response

God's Word always invites a response. Think about the way the theme of divine judgment speaks to us today. How does it invite us to respond?

_____

_____

_____

_____

_____

_____

_____

_____

_____

_____

_____

What is your evaluation of yourself based on any or all of the verses found in 2 Peter 2:1–3:18?

_____

_____

_____

_____

_____

_____

_____

_____

_____

_____

_____

_____

_____

The portrayal of
God as merciful and
forgiving is a source
of hope for all sinners
who seek freedom
from the power of sin.